The Library of Small Ecosystems ™

The Ecosystem of an
Apple Tree

Elaine Pascoe   Photography by Dwight Kuhn

The Rosen Publishing Group's
PowerKids Press™
New York

Published in 2003 by The Rosen Publishing Group, Inc.
29 East 21st Street, New York, NY 10010

First Edition

Editor: Nancy MacDonell Smith
Book Design: Michael J. Caroleo

Photo Credits: Photos © Dwight Kuhn.

Pascoe, Elaine.
The ecosystem of an apple tree / Elaine Pascoe.
      p. cm. — (The Library of small ecosystems)
Includes bibliographical references (p.   ).
Summary: Describes the plant and animal life associated with an apple tree, all of which create a miniature, co-dependent ecosystem.
ISBN 0-8239-6304-7 (lib. bdg.)
1. Apples—Ecology—Juvenile literature. 2. Animal ecology—Juvenile literature. [1. Apples—Ecology. 2. Ecology.] I. Title.
QH541.14 .P384 2003
577—dc21
                              2001006160

Manufactured in the United States of America

Contents

The Apple Tree

An apple tree stands in a field. It seems to be alone, but it is not. Insects, birds, and other living things are all around. They find food and make their homes in the tree. The apple tree helps them **survive**. They help the apple tree, too.

The apple tree is the heart of a small **ecosystem**, a community of living and nonliving things. The insects, the birds, and the other living things all belong to this community. Even the air around the tree and the soil beneath it are parts of the ecosystem. Every part of the ecosystem is important.

Left: *This is an apple tree covered with flowers. The tree is just one member of the ecosystem. Other members are birds, earthworms, and even the soil in which the tree grows.*

Apple Blossoms

The apple tree bursts into **bloom** in spring. It is covered with flowers. Bees and other insects come to feed on **nectar**, a sugary liquid in the flowers. As the bees feed, they carry powdery yellow **pollen** from one flower to the next. Pollen is made by the male part of the flower. Tiny grains of pollen land on the **pistil**, the female part at the center of the flower. Then the base of the pistil begins to change. During the summer, it will grow into an apple. In this way, insects help the apple tree make seeds and fruit.

Top Left: *In the springtime an apple tree is covered with blossoms.*
Top Right: *A honeybee feeds on the nectar in an apple blossom.*
Bottom: *Apple blossoms grow in small groups on the tree's branches.*

Bees and other insects carry pollen from flower to flower. When pollen lands on the pistil at the center of an apple blossom, the pistil begins to change into an apple. This process takes several months.

8

This hawk moth is one of the insects that feeds on nectar, a sugary liquid made by the apple tree's flowers.

The apple blossoms wilt and their petals fall away. The base of the wilted flower begins to swell. Over the summer, it will grow into an apple.

Summer Homes

The apple tree is a summer home for many different animals. A mouse makes a nest among the tree's roots. The mouse's babies will be safe and snug there.

Hornets build a nest high in the leafy branches. The nest looks like a ball of paper. Inside, worker hornets care for their queen, her eggs, and her young.

Birds also nest in the tree. A woodpecker may hollow out a nest space inside the trunk using its sharp bill. The woodpecker raises its young in the hollow space. Other birds build nests among the tree's branches.

Top: *Hornets' nests look like balls of crumpled brown paper.*
Bottom: *This mouse and her young have a nest among the tree's roots.*

A Hummingbird's Nest

A hummingbird may build a tiny nest on a branch of the apple tree. The female bird uses bits of plants and other soft materials to make the cup-shaped nest. Then she lays her eggs in it.

When the eggs hatch, the mother bird is busy all day. She visits flowers near the apple tree to collect nectar. Then she flies back to the nest to feed her hungry young chicks. Back and forth she goes, day after day, until the young birds are old enough to fly. The young birds can fly about three weeks after they hatch. Then they leave the apple tree to live on their own.

Top: *A hummingbird's nest is made of plants and other soft materials. The nest is a safe place for the eggs.*
Bottom: *A mother hummingbird feeds her young.*

Many birds nest in the apple tree's branches, but woodpeckers nest in hollows that they make in the tree's trunk.

Young hummingbirds leave the safety of the nest once they are able to fly. This usually happens when they are about three weeks old.

The ruby-throated hummingbird gets its name from the red patch on its throat.

A Moth's Young

One kind of moth that may visit the apple tree is the female **cecropia moth**. The moth lays tiny eggs on the apple leaves. The eggs have a sticky coating that glues them to the leaves.

When the eggs hatch one or two weeks later, caterpillars crawl out. Right away they begin to eat the apple tree's leaves. The caterpillars eat for weeks, growing all the time, until they are several inches (cm) long. Then each caterpillar spins a **cocoon** of silk threads. The caterpillar makes the threads using special body parts. It stays inside the cocoon over the winter while its body slowly changes. When it breaks out of the cocoon the next spring, it is an adult moth.

Top Left: *The cecropia moth's eggs have a coating that glues them to the apple tree's leaves.* Top Right: *Cecropia moth caterpillars crawl all over the apple tree for weeks, eating the tree's leaves.* Bottom Left: *This is a silk cocoon.* Bottom Right: *An adult moth breaks out of the cocoon and prepares to fly away from the tree.*

More Insects in the Apple Tree

Other insects come to the apple tree, too. Beetles lay eggs on the bark. An insect called an **ichneumon fly** lays its eggs on the young, or **larvae**, of the beetles! When the ichneumon fly eggs hatch, the ichneumon fly young feed on the beetle larvae.

Dozens of tent caterpillars may live in the tree. The caterpillars spin a big nest of silk, where they spend the night. The nest looks like a tent, and this is why the insects are called tent caterpillars. During the day they crawl all over the tree, eating leaves. In time they will change into moths. They will eat a lot of leaves first. Tent caterpillars might harm the tree if they eat too many leaves. The tree needs its leaves. Leaves make food for the tree, using the energy in sunlight.

Top: *During the day tent caterpillars crawl all over the apple tree, eating as many leaves as they can.* Bottom: *At night tent caterpillars return to their tent-shaped nest. The nest is made of silk.*

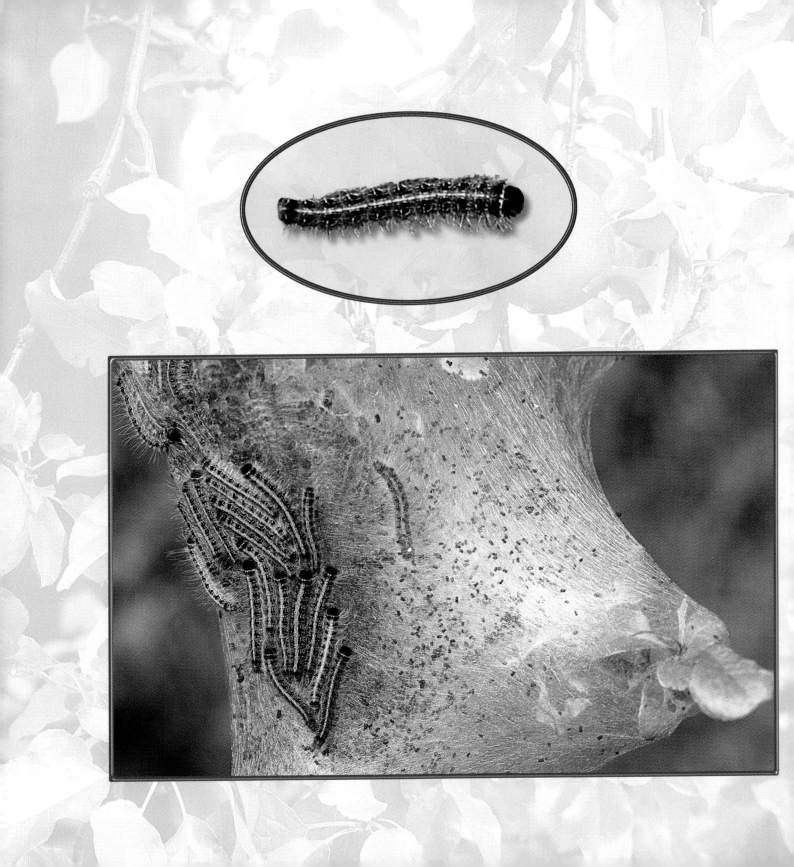

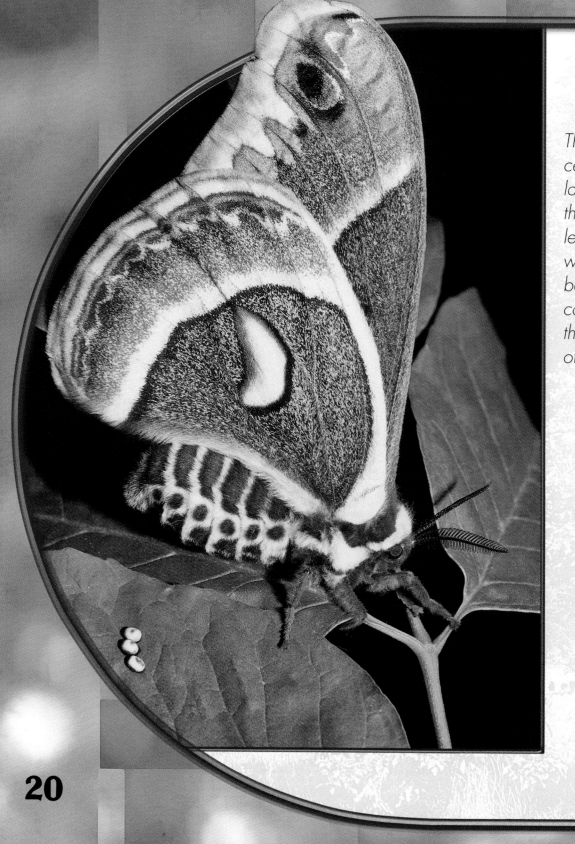

The female cecropia moth lays her eggs on the apple tree's leaves. The eggs will be safe, because a sticky coating keeps them from falling off the leaves.

This is an ichneumon fly laying her eggs on beetle larvae. When the eggs hatch, the ichneumon fly young will eat the beetle larvae.

An insect called an apple psyllid feeds on one of the tree's leaves.

Dinner Guests

Leaf-eating insects are not the only animals that find food in the apple tree. The tree is a place where many kinds of animals can get a meal. A meadow **vole** or a porcupine may chew the bark on the tree's trunk. Birds come to eat caterpillars and other insects.

Even leaves that fall to the ground become food, for earthworms. Earthworms tunnel through the ground under the tree. As they tunnel, they eat bits of dirt, fallen leaves, and other matter. The earthworms **digest** these materials. The worms push out their wastes. This puts **nutrients** into the soil. The tree takes up the nutrients through its roots. In this way earthworms help the apple tree to grow.

Top: *An earthworm pulls a bit of leaf into the soil under the tree.*
Bottom: *A meadow vole snacks on the apple tree's bark.*

Apple Time

The tree's apples ripen in late summer. They grow big and turn red. Their flesh becomes sweet. Then more hungry animals come to the apple tree. Birds, insects, deer, squirrels, and many other animals all want a taste of the tree's fruit. They eat the apples on the tree and the apples that fall to the ground.

Eating a lot of apples helps animals get ready for winter. There won't be much food when winter comes. In late summer many animals eat as much as they can to fatten up before the weather turns cold. Their stored fat will help them stay alive in winter.

Top: *Ripe apples are a treat for the humans, the insects, and the animals who are part of the tree's ecosystem.* Bottom: *A paper wasp feeds on an apple.*

The apple tree provides food for many members of the ecosystem. As do meadow voles, porcupines eat the apple tree's bark. Along with the bark, the apple tree's leaves and fruit and the nectar of its blossoms are all sources of food.

Squirrels and many other animals eat apples that drop from the tree. These animals are important members of the apple tree community. When they eat apples, they help to scatter apple seeds. In this way they help new apple trees to grow.

27

Season's End

By late fall only a few apples are still on the tree. Many have fallen, and many have been eaten. Squirrels hurry around, collecting the last of the apples. Squirrels sometimes store apples in hiding places to eat during the winter.

By eating its fruit, squirrels and other animals help the apple tree. Inside every apple are apple seeds. When animals collect apples and eat them, they scatter the seeds. In spring the seeds **sprout**. New apple trees grow. In time the new trees will provide homes and food for other living things.

Top Left: *Squirrels collect apples and store them to eat during the winter.*
Top Right: *A cut-open apple shows the seeds that might grow into new apple trees.* Bottom: *New seedlings sprout from a rotting apple.*

The Apple-Tree Community

All the members of the apple-tree community depend on one another. The apple tree cannot make seeds or fruit if bees do not come to feed on the nectar of its flowers. The earthworms that eat leaves from the tree improve the soil and help the tree to grow. The animals that eat apples scatter seeds so that new apple trees can sprout.

All living things depend on others to survive. The apple-tree community is just one example of Earth's many ecosystems.

Glossary

bloom (BLOOM) The state of having flowers.

cecropia moth (sih-KROH-pee-uh MAWTH) A large, brown moth with red, white, and black markings.

cocoon (kuh-KOON) A silken case in which a moth caterpillar changes into an adult moth.

digest (dy-JEST) When an animal's body breaks down food to use for energy.

ecosystem (EE-koh-sis-tem) A community of living things and the surroundings, such as air, soil, and water, in which they live.

ichneumon fly (ik-NOO-muhn FLY) A type of insect that lays its eggs in the larvae of other insects.

larvae (LAR-vee) The plural form of larva. The early life stage of certain animals that differs greatly from the adult stage.

nectar (NEK-tur) A sugary liquid in the heart of a flower.

nutrients (NOO-tree-ints) Anything that a living thing needs to live and to grow.

pistil (PIS-tuhl) The female part of a flower.

pollen (PAH-lin) A powder made by the male part of the flower.

sprout (SPROWT) To begin to grow.

survive (sur-VYV) To stay alive.

vole (VOHL) A small animal that is related to mice.

Index

C
cecropia moth, 17
cocoon, 17

E
earthworms, 23, 30
ecosystem(s), 5, 30
eggs, 11–12, 17–18

I
ichneumon fly, 18
insect(s), 5–6, 18,
  23–24

L
larvae, 18

M
mouse, 11

N
nectar, 6, 12, 30
nutrients, 23

P
pistil, 6
pollen, 6

S
seeds, 6, 29–30
spring, 6, 17, 29

T
tent caterpillars, 18

V
vole, 23

W
winter, 17, 24, 29
woodpecker, 11

Web Sites

Due to the changing nature of internet links, PowerKids Press has developed an online list of Web sites related to the subject of this book. This site is updated regularly. Please use this link to access the list.
www.powerkidslinks.com/lse/appleeco/

32